D0977104

ON BULLSHIT

ON BULLSHIT

Harry G. Frankfurt

PRINCETON UNIVERSITY PRESS

PRINCETON AND OXFORD

Copyright © 2005 by Princeton University Press
Published by Princeton University Press,
41 William Street,
Princeton, New Jersey 08540
In the United Kingdom:
Princeton University Press,
3 Market Place, Woodstock,
Oxfordshire OX20 1SY

Frankfurt, Harry G., 1929–
On bullshit / Harry G. Frankfurt
p.   cm.
Includes bibliographical references.
ISBN 0-691-12294-6 (alk. paper)
1. Truthfulness and falsehood. I. Title.
BJ1421.F73   2005
177′.3—dc22   2004058963

British Library Cataloging-in-Publication Data
is available
This book has been composed in Minion
Printed on acid-free paper. ∞
pup.princeton.edu
Printed in the United States of America

13 15 17 19 20 18 16 14 12

To Joan, truly

ON BULLSHIT

One of the most salient features of our culture is that there is so much bullshit. Everyone knows this. Each of us contributes his share. But we tend to take the situation for granted. Most people are rather confident of their ability to recognize bullshit and to avoid being taken in by it. So the phenomenon has not aroused much deliberate concern, nor attracted much sustained inquiry.

In consequence, we have no clear understanding of what bullshit is, why there is so much of it, or what functions it serves. And we lack a conscientiously developed appreciation of what it means to us. In other words, we have no theory. I propose to begin the devel-

opment of a theoretical understanding
of bullshit, mainly by providing some
tentative and exploratory philosophical
analysis. I shall not consider the rhetorical uses and misuses of bullshit. My
aim is simply to give a rough account
of what bullshit is and how it differs
from what it is not—or (putting it
somewhat differently) to articulate,
more or less sketchily, the structure
of its concept.

Any suggestion about what conditions are logically both necessary and
sufficient for the constitution of bullshit
is bound to be somewhat arbitrary.
For one thing, the expression *bullshit*
is often employed quite loosely—simply
as a generic term of abuse, with no very
specific literal meaning. For another,

the phenomenon itself is so vast and amorphous that no crisp and perspicuous analysis of its concept can avoid being procrustean. Nonetheless it should be possible to say something helpful, even though it is not likely to be decisive. Even the most basic and preliminary questions about bullshit remain, after all, not only unanswered but unasked.

So far as I am aware, very little work has been done on this subject. I have not undertaken a survey of the literature, partly because I do not know how to go about it. To be sure, there is one quite obvious place to look—the *Oxford English Dictionary.* The *OED* has an entry for *bullshit* in the supplementary volumes, and it also has entries

for various pertinent uses of the word
bull and for some related terms. I
shall consider some of these entries in
due course. I have not consulted diction-
aries in languages other than English,
because I do not know the words for
bullshit or bull in any other language.
Another worthwhile source is the title
essay in *The Prevalence of Humbug* by
Max Black.[1] I am uncertain just how
close in meaning the word *humbug* is
to the word *bullshit*. Of course, the
words are not freely and fully inter-
changeable; it is clear that they are used
differently. But the difference appears
on the whole to have more to do with

[1] Max Black, *The Prevalence of Humbug* (Ithaca:
Cornell University Press, 1985).

considerations of gentility, and certain
other rhetorical parameters, than with
the strictly literal modes of significance
that concern me most. It is more polite,
as well as less intense, to say "Humbug!" than to say "Bullshit!" For the
sake of this discussion, I shall assume
that there is no other important difference between the two.

Black suggests a number of synonyms
for *humbug*, including the following:
*balderdash, claptrap, hokum, drivel, bun-
combe, imposture,* and *quackery.* This list
of quaint equivalents is not very helpful.
But Black also confronts the problem of
establishing the nature of humbug more
directly, and he offers the following for-
mal definition:

> HUMBUG: deceptive misrepresentation, short of lying, especially by pretentious word or deed, of somebody's own thoughts, feelings, or attitudes.[2]

A very similar formulation might plausibly be offered as enunciating the essential characteristics of bullshit. As a preliminary to developing an independent account of those characteristics, I will comment on the various elements of Black's definition.

Deceptive misrepresentation: This may sound pleonastic. No doubt what Black has in mind is that humbug is necessarily designed or intended to deceive, that its misrepresentation is not merely

[2] Ibid., p. 143.

inadvertent. In other words, it is *deliberate* misrepresentation. Now if, as a matter of conceptual necessity, an intention to deceive is an invariable feature of humbug, then the property of being humbug depends at least in part upon the perpetrator's state of mind. It cannot be identical, accordingly, with any properties—either inherent or relational—belonging just to the utterance by which the humbug is perpetrated. In this respect, the property of being humbug is similar to that of being a lie, which is identical neither with the falsity nor with any of the other properties of the statement the liar makes, but which requires that the liar makes his statement in a certain state of mind—namely, with an intention to deceive.

It is a further question whether there are any features essential to humbug or to lying that are *not* dependent upon the intentions and beliefs of the person responsible for the humbug or the lie, or whether it is, on the contrary, possible for any utterance whatsoever to be—given that the speaker is in a certain state of mind—a vehicle of humbug or of a lie. In some accounts of lying there is no lie unless a false statement is made; in others a person may be lying even if the statement he makes is true, as long as he himself believes that the statement is false and intends by making it to deceive. What about humbug and bullshit? May any utterance at all qualify as humbug or bullshit, given that (so to speak) the utterer's heart is in the right place, or must the utterance have certain characteristics of its own as well?

Short of lying: It must be part of the point of saying that humbug is "short of lying" that while it has some of the distinguishing characteristics of lies, there are others that it lacks. But this cannot be the whole point. After all, every use of language without exception has some, but not all, of the characteristic features of lies—if no other, then at least the feature simply of being a use of language. Yet it would surely be incorrect to describe every use of language as short of lying. Black's phrase evokes the notion of some sort of continuum, on which lying occupies a certain segment while humbug is located exclusively at earlier points. What continuum could this be, along which one encounters humbug only before one encounters lying? Both lying and humbug are modes of misrepresentation. It is not at first glance apparent, however, just how the difference between these varieties of misrepresentation might be construed as a difference in degree.

Especially by pretentious word or deed: There are two points to notice here. First, Black identifies humbug not only as a category of speech but as a category of action as well; it may be accomplished either by words or by deeds. Second, his use of the qualifier "especially" indicates that Black does not regard pretentiousness as an essential or wholly indispensable characteristic of humbug. Undoubtedly, much humbug is pretentious. So far as concerns bullshit, moreover, "pretentious bullshit" is close to being a stock phrase. But I am inclined to think that when bullshit is pretentious, this happens because pretentiousness is its motive rather than a constitutive element of its essence. The fact that a person is behaving pretentiously is not, it seems to me, part of what is required to make his utterance an instance of bullshit. It is often, to be sure, what accounts for his making that utterance. However, it must not be assumed that bullshit always and necessarily has pretentiousness as its motive.

Misrepresentation . . . of somebody's own thoughts, feelings, or attitudes: This provision that the perpetrator of humbug is essentially misrepresenting himself raises some very central issues. To begin with, whenever a person deliberately misrepresents *anything*, he must inevitably be misrepresenting his own state of mind. It is possible, of course, for a person to misrepresent that alone—for instance, by pretending to have a desire or a feeling which he does not actually have. But suppose that a person, whether by telling a lie or in another way, misrepresents something else. Then he necessarily misrepresents at least two things. He misrepresents whatever he is talking about—i.e., the state of affairs that is the topic or referent of his discourse—and in doing this he cannot avoid misrepresenting his own mind as well. Thus someone who lies about how much money he has in his pocket both gives an account of the amount of money in his pocket and conveys that he believes this account. If the lie works, then its victim is twice deceived, having one false belief about what is in the liar's pocket and another false belief about what is in the liar's mind.

Now it is unlikely that Black wishes the referent of humbug to be in every instance the state of the speaker's mind. There is no particular reason, after all, why humbug may not be about other things. Black probably means that humbug is not designed primarily to give its audience a false belief about whatever state of affairs may be the topic, but that its primary intention is rather to give its audience a false impression concerning what is going on in the mind of the speaker. Insofar as it is humbug, the creation of this impression is its main purpose and its point.

Understanding Black along these lines suggests a hypothesis to account for his characterization of humbug as "short of lying." If I lie to you about how much money I have, then I do not thereby make an *explicit* assertion concerning my beliefs. Therefore, one might with some plausibility maintain that although in telling the lie I certainly misrepresent what is in my mind, this misrepresentation—as distinct from my misrepresentation of what is in my pocket—is not strictly speaking a lie at all. For I do not come right out with any statement whatever about what is in my mind. Nor does the statement I do affirm—e.g., "I have twenty dollars in my pocket"—imply any statement that attributes a belief to me. On the other hand, it is unquestionable that in so affirming, I provide you with a reasonable basis for making certain judgments about what I believe. In particular, I provide you with a reasonable basis for supposing that I believe I have twenty dollars in my pocket. Since this supposition is by hypothesis false, I do in telling the lie tend to deceive you concerning what is in my mind even though I do not actually tell a lie about that. In this light, it does not seem unnatural or inappropriate to regard me as misrepresenting my own beliefs in a way that is "short of lying."

It is easy to think of familiar situations by which Black's account of humbug appears to be unproblematically confirmed. Consider a Fourth of July orator, who goes on bombastically about "our great and blessed country, whose Founding Fathers under divine guidance created a new beginning for mankind." This is surely humbug. As Black's account suggests, the orator is not lying. He would be lying only if it were his intention to bring about in his audience beliefs that he himself regards as false, concerning such matters as whether our country is great, whether it is blessed, whether the Founders had divine guidance, and whether what they did was in fact to create a new beginning for mankind. But the orator does not really care what his audience thinks about the Founding Fathers, or about the role of the deity in our country's history, or the like. At least, it is not an interest in what anyone thinks about these matters that motivates his speech.

It is clear that what makes Fourth of July oration humbug is not fundamentally that the speaker regards his statements as false. Rather, just as Black's account suggests, the orator intends these statements to convey a certain impression of himself. He is not trying to deceive anyone concerning American history. What he cares about is what people think of *him*. He wants them to think of him as a patriot, as someone who has deep thoughts and feelings about the origins and the mission of our country, who appreciates the importance of religion, who is sensitive to the greatness of our history, whose pride in that history is combined with humility before God, and so on.

Black's account of humbug appears, then, to fit certain paradigms quite snugly. Nonetheless, I do not believe that it adequately or accurately grasps the essential character of bullshit. It is correct to say of bullshit, as he says of humbug, both that it is short of lying and that those who perpetrate it misrepresent themselves in a certain way. But Black's account of these two features is significantly off the mark. I shall next attempt to develop, by considering some biographical material pertaining to Ludwig Wittgenstein, a preliminary but more accurately focused appreciation of just what the central characteristics of bullshit are.

Wittgenstein once said that the following bit of verse by Longfellow could serve him as a motto:[3]

[3] This is reported by Norman Malcolm, in his introduction to *Recollections of Wittgenstein*, ed. R. Rhees (Oxford: Oxford University Press, 1984), p. xiii.

In the elder days of art
Builders wrought with greatest care
Each minute and unseen part,
For the Gods are everywhere.

The point of these lines is clear. In the old days, craftsmen did not cut corners. They worked carefully, and they took care with every aspect of their work. Every part of the product was considered, and each was designed and made to be exactly as it should be. These craftsmen did not relax their thoughtful self-discipline even with respect to features of their work that would ordinarily not be visible. Although no one would notice if those features were not quite right, the craftsmen would be bothered by their consciences. So nothing was swept under the rug. Or, one might perhaps also say, there was no bullshit.

It does seem fitting to construe carelessly made, shoddy goods as in some way analogues of bullshit. But in what way? Is the resemblance that bullshit itself is invariably produced in a careless or self-indulgent manner, that it is never finely crafted, that in the making of it there is never the meticulously attentive concern with detail to which Longfellow alludes? Is the bullshitter by his very nature a mindless slob? Is his product necessarily messy or unrefined? The word *shit* does, to be sure, suggest this. Excrement is not designed or crafted at all; it is merely emitted, or

dumped. It may have a more or less co-
herent shape, or it may not, but it is in
any case certainly not *wrought*.

The notion of carefully wrought bullshit involves, then, a certain inner
strain. Thoughtful attention to detail
requires discipline and objectivity. It en-
tails accepting standards and limitations
that forbid the indulgence of impulse or
whim. It is this selflessness that, in connection with bullshit, strikes us as inap-
posite. But in fact it is not out of the
question at all. The realms of advertis-
ing and of public relations, and the nowadays closely related realm of politics,
are replete with instances of bullshit so
unmitigated that they can serve among
the most indisputable and classic paradigms of the concept. And in these

realms there are exquisitely sophisti-
cated craftsmen who—with the help of
advanced and demanding techniques of
market research, of public opinion poll-
ing, of psychological testing, and so
forth—dedicate themselves tirelessly to
getting every word and image they produce exactly right.

Yet there is something more to be
said about this. However studiously and
conscientiously the bullshitter proceeds,
it remains true that he is also trying to
get away with something. There is
surely in his work, as in the work of the
slovenly craftsman, some kind of laxity
that resists or eludes the demands of a
disinterested and austere discipline. The
pertinent mode of laxity cannot be
equated, evidently, with simple care-

lessness or inattention to detail. I shall attempt in due course to locate it more correctly.

Wittgenstein devoted his philosophical energies largely to identifying and combating what he regarded as insidiously disruptive forms of "nonsense." He was apparently like that in his personal life as well. This comes out in an anecdote related by Fania Pascal, who knew him in Cambridge in the 1930s:

> I had my tonsils out and was in the Evelyn Nursing Home feeling sorry for myself. Wittgenstein called. I croaked: "I feel just like a dog that has been run over." He was disgusted: "You don't know what a dog that has been run over feels like."[4]

[4] Fania Pascal, "Wittgenstein: A Personal Memoir," in Rhees, *Recollections*, pp. 28–29.

Now who knows what really happened?
It seems extraordinary, almost unbeliev-
able, that anyone could object seriously
to what Pascal reports herself as having
said. That characterization of her feelings—so innocently close to the utterly
commonplace "sick as a dog"—is simply not provocative enough to arouse
any response as lively or intense as dis-
gust. If Pascal's simile is offensive, then
what figurative or allusive uses of language would not be?

So perhaps it did not really happen
quite as Pascal says. Perhaps Wittgenstein was trying to make a small
joke, and it misfired. He was only pretending to bawl Pascal out, just for the
fun of a little hyperbole; and she got
the tone and the intention wrong. She

thought he was disgusted by her remark, when in fact he was only trying to cheer her up with some playfully exaggerated mock criticism or joshing. In that case the incident is not incredible or bizarre after all.

But if Pascal failed to recognize that Wittgenstein was only teasing, then perhaps the possibility that he was serious was at least not so far out of the question. She knew him, and she knew what to expect from him; she knew how he made her feel. Her way of understanding or of misunderstanding his remark was very likely not altogether discordant, then, with her sense of what he was like. We may fairly suppose that even if her account of the incident is not strictly true to the facts of Wittgenstein's intention, it is sufficiently true to her idea of Wittgenstein to have made sense to her. For the purposes of this discussion, I shall accept Pascal's report at face value, supposing that when it came to the use of allusive or figurative language, Wittgenstein was indeed as preposterous as she makes him out to be.

Then just what is it that the Wittgenstein in her report considers to be objectionable? Let us assume that he is correct about the facts: that is, Pascal really does not know how run-over dogs feel. Even so, when she says what she does, she is plainly not *lying*. She would have been lying if, when she made her statement, she was aware that she actually felt quite good. For however little she knows about the lives of dogs, it must certainly be clear to Pascal that when dogs are run over they do not feel good. So if she herself had in fact been feeling good, it would have been a lie to assert that she felt like a run-over dog.

Pascal's Wittgenstein intends to accuse her not of lying but of misrepresentation of another sort. She characterizes her feeling as "the feeling of a run-over dog." She is not really acquainted, however, with the feeling to which this phrase refers. Of course, the phrase is far from being complete nonsense to her; she is hardly speaking gibberish. What she says has an intelligible connotation, which she certainly understands. Moreover, she does know something about the quality of the feeling to which the phrase refers: she knows at least that it is an undesirable and unenjoyable feeling, a *bad* feeling. The trouble with her statement is that it purports to convey something more than simply that she feels bad. Her characterization of her feeling is too specific; it is excessively particular. Hers is not just any bad feeling but, according to her account, the distinctive kind of bad feeling that a dog has when it is run over. To the Wittgenstein in Pascal's story, judging from his response, this is just bullshit.

Now assuming that Wittgenstein does indeed regard Pascal's characterization of how she feels as an instance of bullshit, why does it strike him that way? It does so, I believe, because he perceives what Pascal says as being—roughly speaking, for now—unconnected to a concern with the truth. Her statement is not germane to the enterprise of describing reality. She does not even think she knows, except in the vaguest way, how a run-over dog feels. Her description of her own feeling is, accordingly, something that she is merely making up. She concocts it out of whole cloth; or, if she got it from someone else, she is repeating it quite mindlessly and without any regard for how things really are.

It is for this mindlessness that Pascal's Wittgenstein chides her. What disgusts him is that Pascal is not even concerned whether her statement is correct. There is every likelihood, of course, that she says what she does only in a somewhat clumsy effort to speak colorfully, or to appear vivacious or good-humored; and no doubt Wittgenstein's reaction—as she construes it—is absurdly intolerant. Be this as it may, it seems clear what that reaction is. He reacts as though he perceives her to be speaking about her feeling thoughtlessly, without conscientious attention to the relevant facts. Her statement is not "wrought with greatest care." She makes it without bothering to take into account at all the question of its accuracy.

The point that troubles Wittgenstein is manifestly not that Pascal has made a mistake in her description of how she feels. Nor is it even that she has made a careless mistake. Her laxity, or her lack of care, is not a matter of having permit-

ted an error to slip into her speech on
account of some inadvertent or momen-
tarily negligent lapse in the attention
she was devoting to getting things
right. The point is rather that, so far
as Wittgenstein can see, Pascal offers a
description of a certain state of affairs
without genuinely submitting to the
constraints which the endeavor to provide an accurate representation of reality imposes. Her fault is not that she
fails to get things right, but that she is
not even trying.

This is important to Wittgenstein
because, whether justifiably or not, he
takes what she says seriously, as a statement purporting to give an informative
description of the way she feels. He

construes her as engaged in an activity
to which the distinction between what
is true and what is false is crucial, and
yet as taking no interest in whether
what she says is true or false. It is in
this sense that Pascal's statement is unconnected to a concern with truth: she
is not concerned with the truth-value
of what she says. That is why she cannot be regarded as lying; for she does
not presume that she knows the truth,
and therefore she cannot be deliberately
promulgating a proposition that she
presumes to be false: Her statement is
grounded neither in a belief that it is
true nor, as a lie must be, in a belief
that it is not true. It is just this lack of
connection to a concern with truth—

this indifference to how things really are—that I regard as of the essence of bullshit.

Now I shall consider (quite selectively) certain items in the *Oxford English Dictionary* that are pertinent to clarifying the nature of bullshit. The *OED* defines a *bull session* as "an informal conversation or discussion, esp. of a group of males." Now as a definition, this seems wrong. For one thing, the dictionary evidently supposes that the use of the term *bull* in *bull session* serves primarily just to indicate gender. But even if it were true that the participants in bull sessions are generally or typically males, the assertion that a bull session is essentially nothing more particular than an informal discussion among

males would be as far off the mark as
the parallel assertion that a hen session
is simply an informal conversation
among females. It is probably true that
the participants in hen sessions must be
females. Nonetheless the term *hen session* conveys something more specific
than this concerning the particular kind
of informal conversation among females
to which hen sessions are characteristi-
cally devoted. What is distinctive about
the sort of informal discussion among
males that constitutes a bull session is,
it seems to me, something like this:
while the discussion may be intense
and significant, it is in a certain respect
not "for real."

The characteristic topics of a bull session have to do with very personal and

emotion-laden aspects of life—for instance, religion, politics, or sex. People are generally reluctant to speak altogether openly about these topics if they expect that they might be taken too seriously. What tends to go on in a bull session is that the participants try out various thoughts and attitudes in order to see how it feels to hear themselves saying such things and in order to discover how others respond, without its being assumed that they are committed to what they say: it is understood by everyone in a bull session that the statements people make do not necessarily reveal what they really believe or how they really feel. The main point is to make possible a high level of candor and an experimental or adventuresome approach to the subjects under discussion. Therefore provision is made for enjoying a certain irresponsibility, so that people will be encouraged to convey what is on their minds without too much anxiety that they will be held to it.

Each of the contributors to a bull session relies, in other words, upon a general recognition that what he expresses or says is not to be understood as being what he means wholeheartedly or believes unequivocally to be true. The purpose of the conversation is not to communicate beliefs. Accordingly, the usual assumptions about the connection between what people say and what they believe are suspended. The statements

made in a bull session differ from bullshit in that there is no pretense that this
connection is being sustained. They are
like bullshit by virtue of the fact that
they are in some degree unconstrained
by a concern with truth. This resemblance between bull sessions and bullshit is suggested also by the term *shooting the bull,* which refers to the sort of
conversation that characterizes bull
sessions and in which the term *shooting*
is very likely a cleaned-up rendition of
shitting. The very term *bull session* is, indeed, quite probably a sanitized version
of *bullshit session.*

A similar theme is discernible in a
British usage of *bull* in which, according
to the *OED,* the term refers to "unneces-

sary routine tasks or ceremonial; excessive discipline or 'spit-and-polish'; = red-tape." The dictionary provides the following examples of this usage:

> The Squadron . . . felt very bolshie about all that bull that was flying around the station (I. Gleed, *Arise to Conquer* vi. 51, 1942); Them turning out the guard for us, us marching past eyes right, all that sort of bull (A. Baron, *Human Kind* xxiv. 178, 1953); the drudgery and 'bull' in an MP's life (*Economist* 8 Feb. 470/471, 1958).

Here the term *bull* evidently pertains to tasks that are pointless in that they have nothing much to do with the primary intent or justifying purpose of the enterprise which requires them. Spit-and-polish and red tape do not genuinely contribute, it is presumed, to the "real" purposes of military personnel or government officials, even though they are imposed by agencies or agents that purport to be conscientiously devoted to the pursuit of those purposes. Thus the "unnecessary routine tasks or cere-monial" that constitute bull are discon-nected from the legitimating motives of the activity upon which they intrude, just as the things people say in bull sessions are disconnected from their settled beliefs, and as bullshit is dis-connected from a concern with the truth.

The term *bull* is also employed, in a rather more widespread and familiar usage, as a somewhat less coarse equivalent of *bullshit*. In an entry for *bull* as so used, the *OED* suggests the following as definitive: "trivial, insincere, or untruthful talk or writing; nonsense." Now it does not seem distinctive of bull either that it must be deficient in meaning or that it is necessarily unimportant; so "nonsense" and "trivial," even apart from their vagueness, seem to be on the wrong track. The focus of "insincere, or untruthful" is better, but it needs to be sharpened.[5] The entry at hand also provides the following two definitions:

> 1914 Dialect Notes IV. 162 Bull, talk which is not to the purpose; 'hot air'.

[5] It may be noted that the inclusion of insincerity among its essential conditions would imply that bull cannot be produced inadvertently; for it hardly seems possible to be inadvertently insincere.

1932 Times Lit. Supp. 8 Dec. 933/3 'Bull' is the slang term for a combination of bluff, bravado, 'hot air', and what we used to call in the Army 'Kidding the troops'.

"Not to the purpose" is appropriate, but it is both too broad in scope and too vague. It covers digressions and innocent irrelevancies, which are not invariably instances of bull; furthermore, saying that bull is not to the purpose leaves it uncertain what purpose is meant. The reference in both definitions to "hot air" is more helpful.

When we characterize talk as hot air, we mean that what comes out of the speaker's mouth is only that. It is mere vapor. His speech is empty, without substance or content. His use of language, accordingly, does not contribute to the purpose it purports to serve. No more information is communicated than if the speaker had merely exhaled. There are similarities between hot air and excrement, incidentally, which make *hot air* seem an especially suitable equivalent for *bullshit*. Just as hot air is speech that has been emptied of all informative content, so excrement is matter from which everything nutritive has been removed. Excrement may be regarded as the corpse of nourishment, what remains when the vital elements in food have been exhausted. In this respect, excrement is a representation of death that we ourselves produce and that, indeed, we cannot help producing in the very process of maintaining our lives. Perhaps it is for making death so intimate that we find excrement so repulsive. In any event, it cannot serve the purposes of sustenance, any more than hot air can serve those of communication.

Now consider these lines from Pound's Canto LXXIV, which the *OED* cites in its entry on *bullshit* as a verb:

> Hey Snag wots in the bibl'?
> Wot are the books ov the bible?
> Name 'em, don't bullshit ME.[6]

---

[6] Here is part of the context in which these lines occur: "Les Albigeois, a problem of history, / and the fleet at Salamis made with money lent by the state to the shipwrights / Tempus tacendi, tempus loquendi. / Never inside the country to raise the standard of living / but always abroad to increase the profits of usurers, / dixit Lenin, / and gun sales lead to more gun sales / they do not clutter the market for gunnery / there is no saturation / Pisa, in

This is a call for the facts. The person
addressed is evidently regarded as
having in some way claimed to know
the Bible, or as having claimed to care
about it. The speaker suspects that
this is just empty talk, and demands
that the claim be supported with facts.
He will not accept a mere report; he
insists upon seeing the thing itself. In
other words, he is calling the bluff.
The connection between bullshit and
bluff is affirmed explicitly in the definition with which the lines by Pound are
associated:

---

the 23rd year of the effort in sight of the tower /
and Till was hung yesterday / for murder and rape
with trimmings plus Cholkis / plus mythology,
thought he was Zeus ram or another one / Hey
Snag wots in the bibl'? / Wot are the books ov the
bible? / Name 'em, don't bullshit ME."

As v. *trans.* and *intr.*, to talk nonsense
(to); . . . also, to bluff *one's way through*
(something) by talking nonsense.

It does seem that bullshitting involves
a kind of bluff. It is closer to bluffing,
surely, than to telling a lie. But what is
implied concerning its nature by the
fact that it is more like the former than
it is like the latter? Just what is the relevant difference here between a bluff
and a lie?

Lying and bluffing are both modes
of misrepresentation or deception. Now
the concept most central to the distinctive nature of a lie is that of falsity: the
liar is essentially someone who deliberately promulgates a falsehood. Bluffing,
too, is typically devoted to conveying

something false. Unlike plain lying, however, it is more especially a matter not of falsity but of fakery. This is what accounts for its nearness to bullshit. For the essence of bullshit is not that it is *false* but that it is *phony*. In order to appreciate this distinction, one must recognize that a fake or a phony need not be in any respect (apart from authenticity itself) inferior to the real thing. What is not genuine need not also be defective in some other way. It may be, after all, an exact copy. What is wrong with a counterfeit is not what it is like, but how it was made. This points to a similar and fundamental aspect of the essential nature of bullshit: although it is produced without concern with the truth, it need not be false. The bullshitter is faking things. But this does not mean that he necessarily gets them wrong.

In Eric Ambler's novel *Dirty Story*, a character named Arthur Abdel Simpson recalls advice that he received as a child from his father:

> Although I was only seven when my father was killed, I still remember him very well and some of the things he used to say. . . . One of the first things he taught me was, "*Never tell a lie when you can bullshit your way through.*"[7]

[7] E. Ambler, *Dirty Story* (1967), I. iii. 25. The citation is provided in the same *OED* entry as the one that includes the passage from Pound. The closeness of the relation between bullshitting and bluffing is resonant, it seems to me, in the parallelism of the idioms: "bullshit your way through" and "bluff your way through."

This presumes not only that there is an important difference between lying and bullshitting, but that the latter is preferable to the former. Now the elder Simpson surely did not consider bullshitting morally superior to lying. Nor is it likely that he regarded lies as invariably less effective than bullshit in accomplishing the purposes for which either of them might be employed. After all, an intelligently crafted lie may do its work with unqualified success. It may be that Simpson thought it easier to get away with bullshitting than with lying. Or perhaps he meant that, although the risk of being caught is about the same in each case, the consequences of being caught are generally less severe for the bullshitter than for the liar. In fact, people do tend to be more tolerant of bullshit than of lies, perhaps because we are less inclined to take the former as a personal affront. We may seek to distance ourselves from bullshit, but we are more likely to turn away from it with an impatient or irritated shrug than with the sense of violation or outrage that lies often inspire. The problem of understanding why our attitude toward bullshit is generally more benign than our attitude toward lying is an important one, which I shall leave as an exercise for the reader.

The pertinent comparison is not, however, between telling a lie and producing some particular instance of bullshit. The elder Simpson identifies the alternative to telling a lie as "bull-shitting one's way through." This involves not merely producing one instance of bullshit; it involves a *program* of producing bullshit to whatever extent the circumstances require. This is a key, perhaps, to his preference. Telling a lie is an act with a sharp focus. It is designed to insert a particular falsehood at a specific point in a set or system of beliefs, in order to avoid the consequences of having that point occupied by the truth. This requires a degree of craftsmanship, in which the teller of the lie submits to objective constraints imposed by what he takes to be the truth. The liar is inescapably concerned with truth-values. In order to invent a lie at all, he must think he knows what is true. And in order to invent an effective lie, he must design his falsehood under the guidance of that truth.

On the other hand, a person who undertakes to bullshit his way through has much more freedom. His focus is panoramic rather than particular. He does not limit himself to inserting a certain falsehood at a specific point, and thus he is not constrained by the truths surrounding that point or intersecting it. He is prepared, so far as required, to fake the context as well. This freedom from the constraints to which the liar must submit does not necessarily mean, of course, that his task is easier than the task of the liar. But the mode of creativity upon which it relies is less analytical and less deliberative than that which is mobilized in lying. It is more expansive and independent, with more spacious opportunities for improvisation, color, and imaginative play. This is less a matter of craft than of art. Hence the familiar notion of the "bullshit artist." My guess is that the recommendation offered by Arthur Simpson's father reflects the fact that he was more strongly drawn to this mode of creativity, regardless of its relative merit or effectiveness, than he was to the more austere and rigorous demands of lying.

What bullshit essentially misrepresents is neither the state of affairs to which it refers nor the beliefs of the speaker concerning that state of affairs.

Those are what lies misrepresent, by virtue of being false. Since bullshit need not be false, it differs from lies in its misrepresentational intent. The bullshitter may not deceive us, or even intend to do so, either about the facts or about what he takes the facts to be. What he does necessarily attempt to deceive us about is his enterprise. His only indispensably distinctive characteristic is that in a certain way he misrepresents what he is up to.

This is the crux of the distinction between him and the liar. Both he and the liar represent themselves falsely as endeavoring to communicate the truth. The success of each depends upon deceiving us about that. But the fact about himself that the liar hides is that he is attempting to lead us away from a correct apprehension of reality; we are not to know that he wants us to believe something he supposes to be false. The fact about himself that the bullshitter hides, on the other hand, is that the truth-values of his statements are of no central interest to him; what we are not to understand is that his intention is neither to report the truth nor to conceal it. This does not mean that his speech is anarchically impulsive, but that the motive guiding and controlling it is unconcerned with how the things about which he speaks truly are.

It is impossible for someone to lie unless he thinks he knows the truth. Producing bullshit requires no such conviction. A person who lies is thereby responding to the truth, and he is to that extent respectful of it. When an honest man speaks, he says only what he believes to be true; and for the liar, it is correspondingly indispensable that he considers his statements to be false. For the bullshitter, however, all these bets are off: he is neither on the side of the true nor on the side of the false. His eye is not on the facts at all, as the eyes of the honest man and of the liar are, except insofar as they may be pertinent to his interest in getting away with what he says. He does not care whether the things he says describe reality correctly. He just picks them out, or makes them up, to suit his purpose.

In his essay "Lying," Saint Augustine distinguishes lies of eight types, which he classifies according to the characteristic intent or justification with which a lie is told. Lies of seven of these types are told only because they are supposed to be indispensable means to some end that is distinct from the sheer creation of false beliefs. It is not their falsity as such, in other words, that attracts the teller to them. Since they are told only on account of their supposed indispensability to a goal other than deception itself, Saint Augustine regards them as being told unwillingly: what the person really wants is not to tell the lie but to attain the goal. They are therefore not real lies, in his view, and those who tell them are not in the strictest sense liars. It is only the remaining category that contains what he identifies as "the lie which is told solely for the pleasure of lying and deceiving, that is, the real lie."[8] Lies in this category are not told as means to any end distinct from the propagation of falsehood. They are told simply for their own sakes—i.e., purely out of a love of deception:

> There is a distinction between a person who tells a lie and a liar. The former is one who tells a lie unwillingly, while the liar loves to lie and passes his time in the joy of lying. . . . The latter takes delight in lying, rejoicing in the falsehood itself.[9]

[8] "Lying," in *Treatises on Various Subjects*, in *Fathers of the Church*, ed. R. J. Deferrari, vol. 16 (New York: Fathers of the Church, 1952), p. 109. Saint Augustine maintains that telling a lie of this type is a less serious sin than telling lies in three of his categories and a more serious sin than telling lies in the other four categories.

[9] Ibid., p. 79.

What Augustine calls "liars" and "real lies" are both rare and extraordinary. Everyone lies from time to time, but there are very few people to whom it would often (or even ever) occur to lie exclusively from a love of falsity or of deception.

For most people, the fact that a statement is false constitutes in itself a reason, however weak and easily overridden, not to make the statement. For Saint Augustine's pure liar it is, on the contrary, a reason in favor of making it. For the bullshitter it is in itself neither a reason in favor nor a reason against. Both in lying and in telling the truth people are guided by their beliefs concerning the way things are. These guide them as they endeavor either to describe the world correctly or to describe it deceitfully. For this reason, telling lies does not tend to unfit a person for telling the truth in the same way that bullshitting tends to. Through excessive indulgence in the latter activity, which involves making assertions without paying attention to anything except what it suits one to say, a person's normal habit of attending to the ways things are may become attenuated or lost. Someone who lies and someone who tells the truth are playing on opposite sides, so to speak, in the same game. Each responds to the facts as he understands them, although the response of the one is guided by the authority of the truth, while the response of the other defies that authority and refuses to meet its demands. The bullshitter ignores these demands altogether. He does not reject the authority of the truth, as the liar does, and oppose himself to it. He pays no attention to it at all. By virtue of this, bullshit is a greater enemy of the truth than lies are.

One who is concerned to report or to conceal the facts assumes that there are indeed facts that are in some way both determinate and knowable. His interest in telling the truth or in lying presupposes that there is a difference between getting things wrong and getting them right, and that it is at least occasionally possible to tell the difference. Someone who ceases to believe in the possibility of identifying certain statements as true and others as false can have only two alternatives. The first is to desist both from efforts to tell the truth and from efforts to deceive. This would mean refraining from making any assertion whatever about the facts. The second alternative is to continue making assertions that purport to describe the way things are, but that cannot be anything except bullshit.

Why is there so much bullshit? Of course it is impossible to be sure that there is relatively more of it nowadays than at other times. There is more communication of all kinds in our time than ever before, but the proportion that is bullshit may not have increased. Without assuming that the incidence of bullshit is actually greater now, I will mention a few considerations that help to account for the fact that it is currently so great.

Bullshit is unavoidable whenever circumstances require someone to talk without knowing what he is talking about. Thus the production of bullshit is stimulated whenever a person's obligations or opportunities to speak about some topic exceed his knowledge of the facts that are relevant to that topic. This discrepancy is common in public life, where people are frequently impelled—whether by their own propensities or by the demands of others—to speak extensively about matters of which they are to some degree ignorant. Closely related instances arise from the widespread conviction that it is the responsibility of a citizen in a democracy to have opinions about everything, or at least everything that pertains to the conduct of his country's affairs. The lack of any significant connection between a person's opinions and his apprehension of reality will be even more severe, needless to say, for someone who believes it his responsibility, as a conscientious moral agent, to evaluate events and conditions in all parts of the world.

The contemporary proliferation of bullshit also has deeper sources, in various forms of skepticism which deny that we can have any reliable access to an objective reality, and which therefore reject the possibility of knowing how things truly are. These "antirealist" doctrines undermine confidence in the value of disinterested efforts to determine what is true and what is false, and even in the intelligibility of the notion of objective inquiry. One response to this loss of confidence has been a retreat from the discipline required by dedication to the ideal of *correctness* to a quite different sort of discipline, which is imposed by pursuit of an alternative ideal of *sincerity*. Rather than seeking primarily to arrive at accurate representations of a common world, the individual turns toward trying to provide honest representations of himself. Convinced that reality has no inherent nature, which he might hope to identify as the truth about things, he devotes himself to being true to his own nature. It is as though he decides that since it makes no sense to try to be true to the facts, he must therefore try instead to be true to himself.

But it is preposterous to imagine that we ourselves are determinate, and hence susceptible both to correct and to incorrect descriptions, while supposing that the ascription of determinacy to anything else has been exposed as a mistake. As conscious beings, we exist only in response to other things, and we cannot know ourselves at all without knowing them. Moreover, there is nothing in theory, and certainly nothing in experience, to support the extraordinary judgment that it is the truth about himself that is the easiest for a person to know. Facts about ourselves are not peculiarly

solid and resistant to skeptical dissolu-
tion. Our natures are, indeed, elusively
insubstantial—notoriously less stable
and less inherent than the natures of
other things. And insofar as this is the
case, sincerity itself is bullshit.

ABOUT THE AUTHOR

Harry G. Frankfurt, renowned moral philosopher, is Professor of Philosophy Emeritus at Princeton University. His books include *The Reasons of Love* (Princeton), *Necessity, Volition, and Love*, and *The Importance of What We Care About*.